# Art Nouveau Fashions
## Coloring Book

## Ming-Ju Sun

DOVER PUBLICATIONS, INC.
Mineola, New York

# NOTE

The thirty-one exquisitely drawn illustration plates in this stunning collection epitomize the beauty and grace of the Art Nouveau period. Noted artist Ming-Ju Sun presents an array of fashions set among—and incorporating—diverse elements of nature. Flowers and vines, as well as birds, cats, and dogs, and even adorable fairies, adorn these pages inspired by women's styles of the 1890s to the early 1900s. The charming models wear hats and jewelry that add to the pleasure of coloring the extraordinarily detailed images.

*Copyright*
Copyright © 2013 by Ming-Ju Sun
All rights reserved.

*Bibliographical Note*
*Creative Haven Art Nouveau Fashions Coloring Book* is a new work,
first published by Dover Publications, Inc., in 2013.

*International Standard Book Number*
ISBN-13: 978-0-486-49211-7
ISBN-10: 0-486-49211-7

Manufactured in the United States by RR Donnelley
49211709    2015
www.doverpublications.com